BIG NOTE PIANO

Christmas Songs for Kids

Second Edition

CONTENTS

ISBN 978-0-7935-1472-4

HAL•LEONARD®
CORPORATION

7777 W. BLUEMOUND RD. P.O. BOX 13819 MILWAUKEE, WI 53213

Visit Hal Leonard Online at

www.halleonard.com

DO YOU WANT TO BUILD A SNOWMAN?

from FROZEN

Music and Lyrics by KRISTEN ANDERSON-LOPEZ
and ROBERT LOPEZ

FROSTY THE SNOW MAN

Words and Music by STEVE NELSON
and JACK ROLLINS

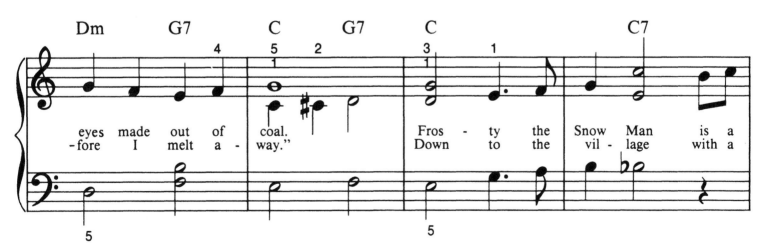

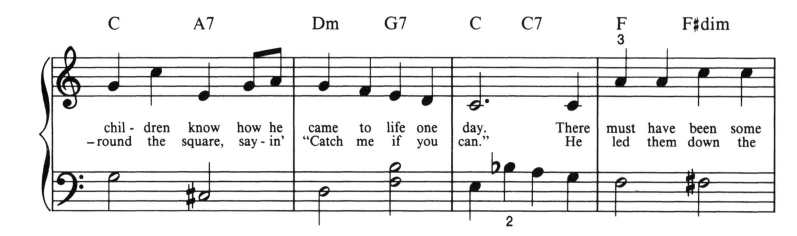

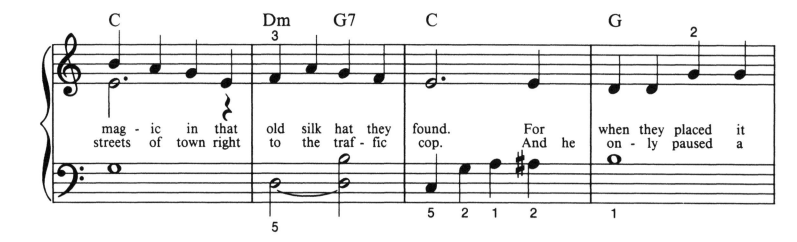

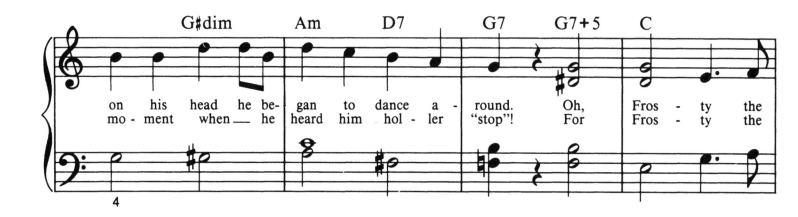

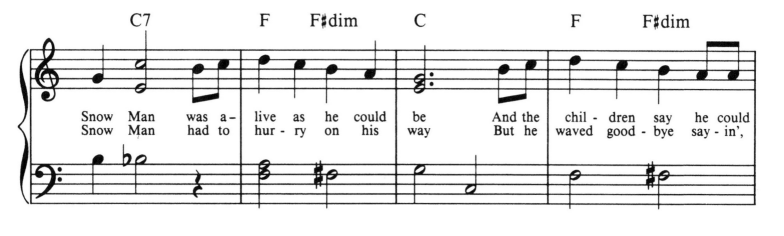

Snow Man was a- live as he could be And the chil - dren say he could
Snow Man had to hur - ry on his way But he waved good - bye say - in',

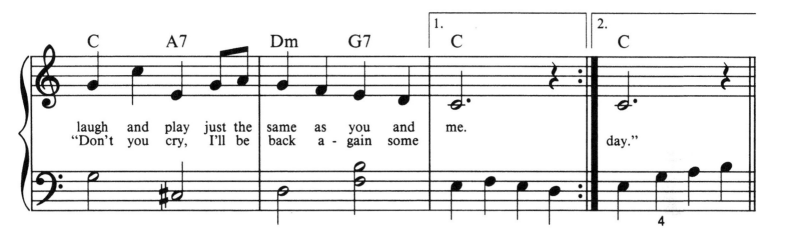

laugh and play just the same as you and me.
"Don't you cry, I'll be back a - gain some day."

Thump-et - y thump thump, thump-et - y thump thump Look at Fros - ty go.

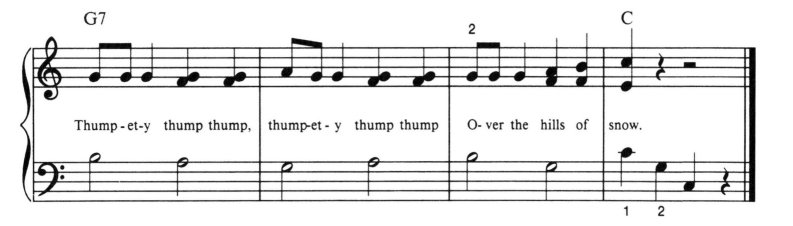

Thump-et - y thump thump, thump-et - y thump thump O- ver the hills of snow.

THE CHIPMUNK SONG

Words and Music by
ROSS BAGDASARIAN

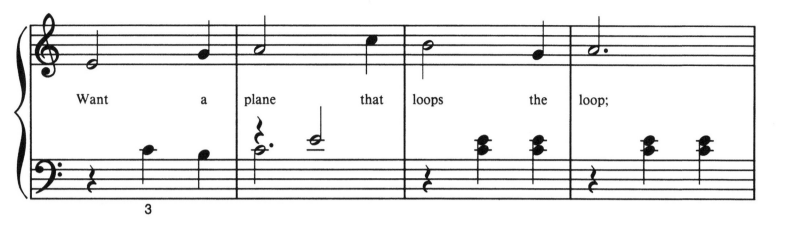

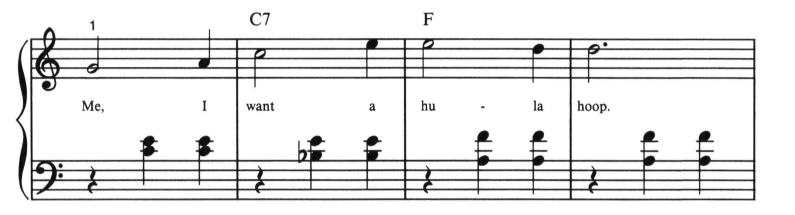

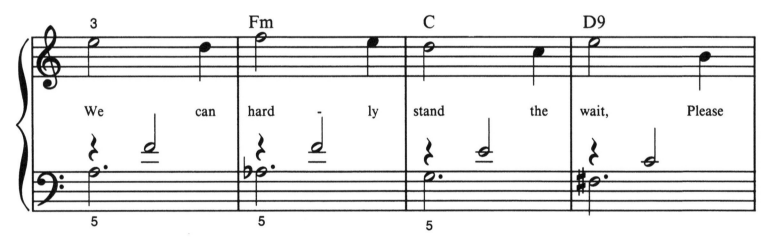

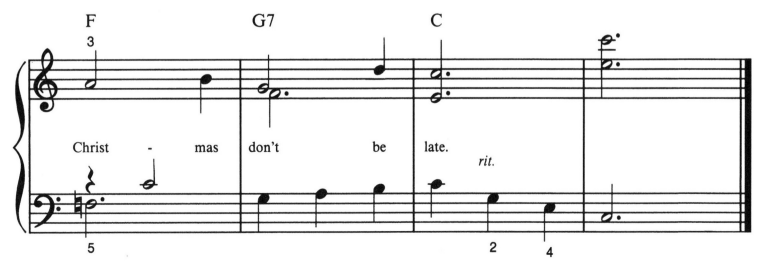

DECK THE HALL

Welsh

With Spirit

Deck the hall with
See the blaz - ing

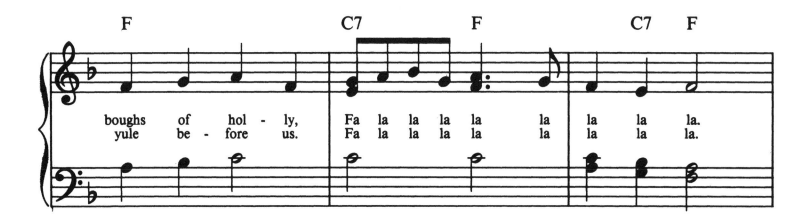

boughs of hol - ly,
yule be - fore us.

Fa la la la la la la la la.
Fa la la la la la la la la.

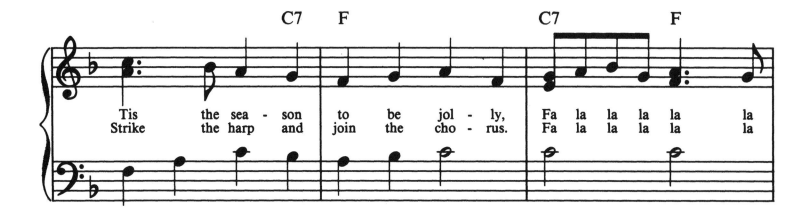

Tis the sea - son to be jol - ly,
Strike the harp and join the cho - rus.

Fa la la la la la
Fa la la la la la

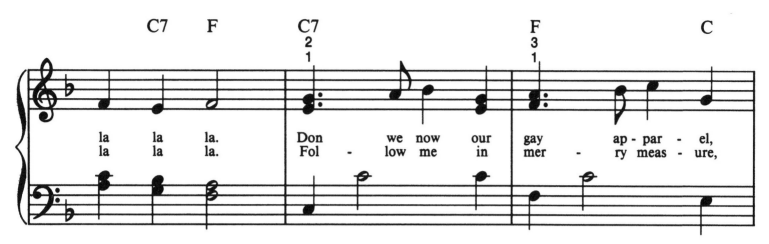

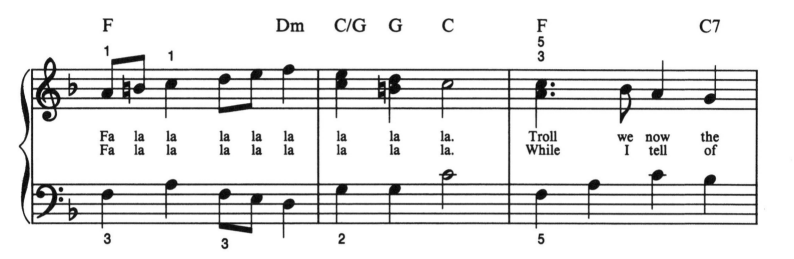

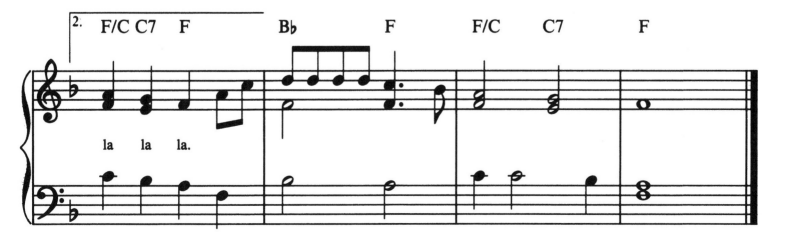

THE FIRST NOEL

French-English

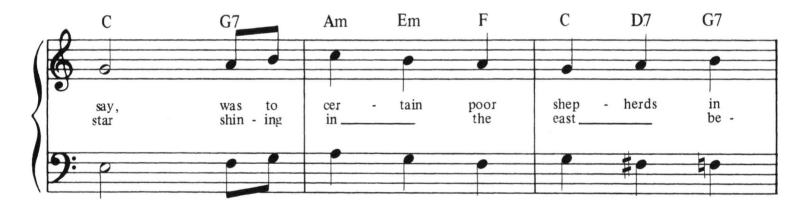

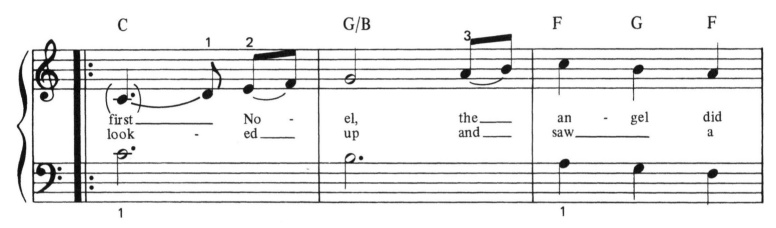

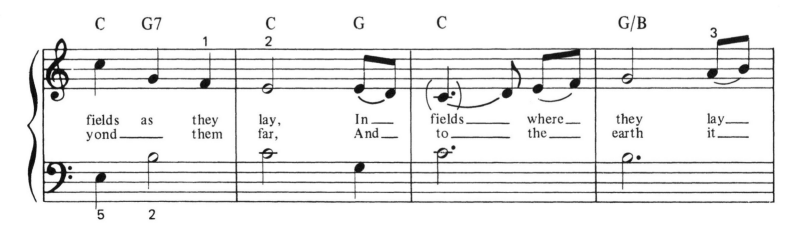

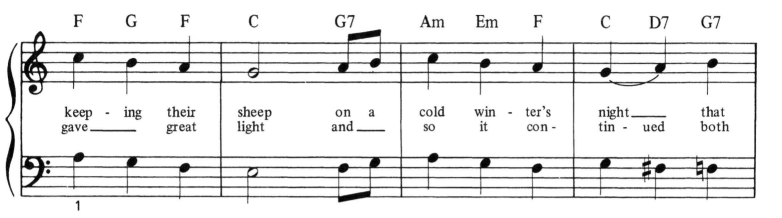

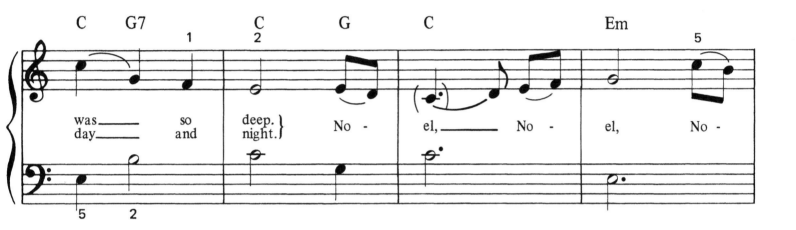

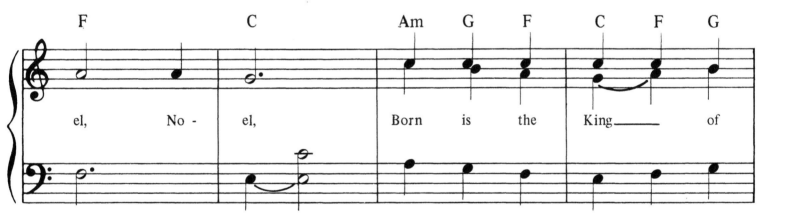

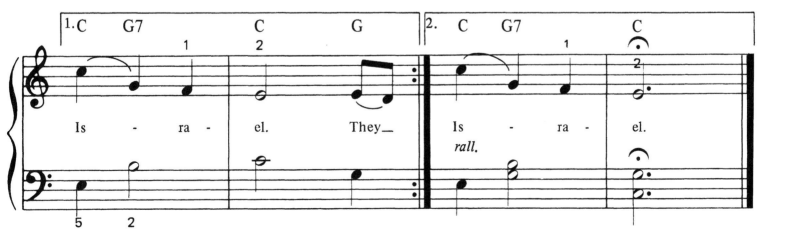

HARK! THE HERALD ANGELS SING

Words by CHARLES WESLEY
Music by FELIX MENDELSSOHN-BARTHOLDY

13

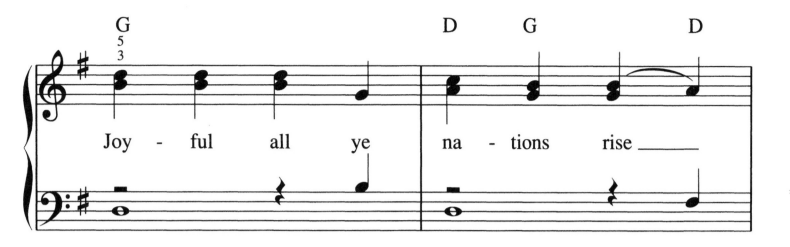

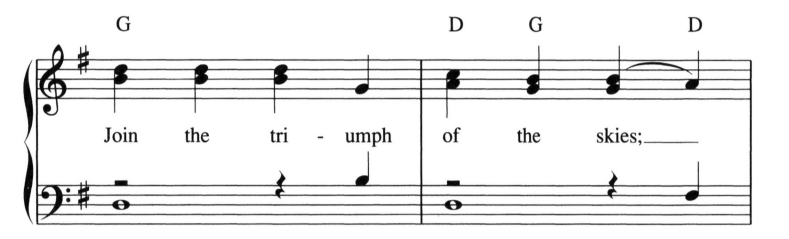

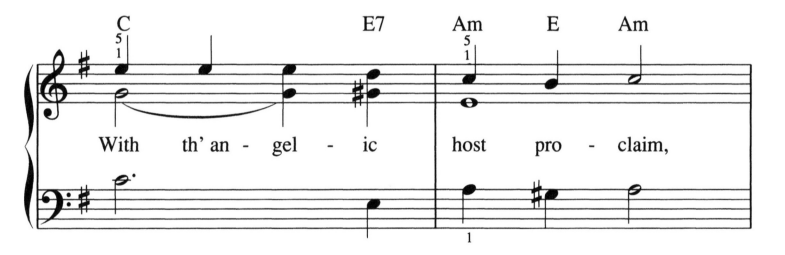

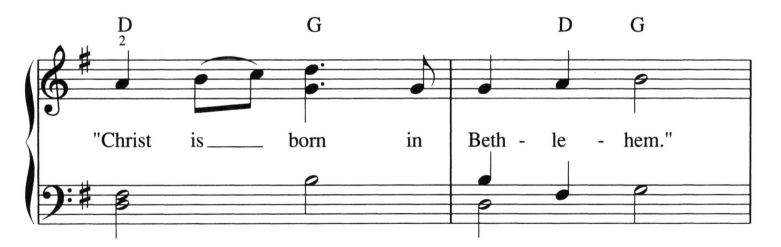

14

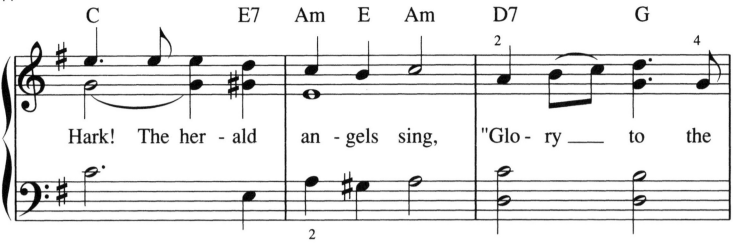

Hark! The her - ald an - gels sing, "Glo - ry ___ to the

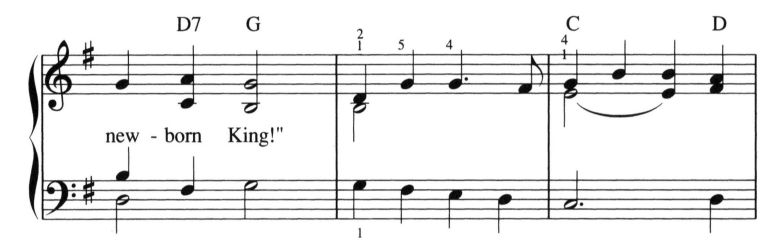

new - born King!"

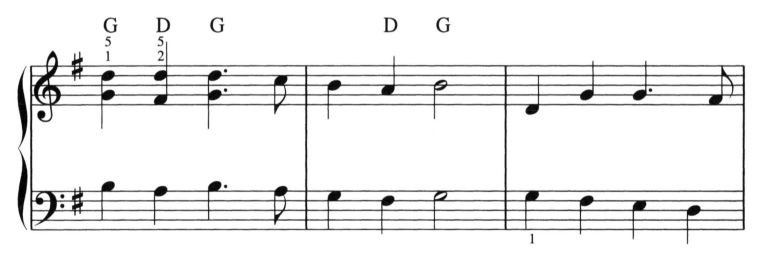

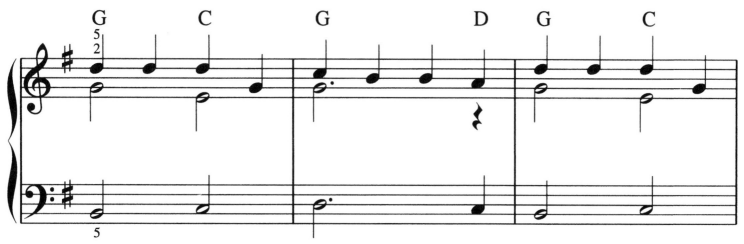

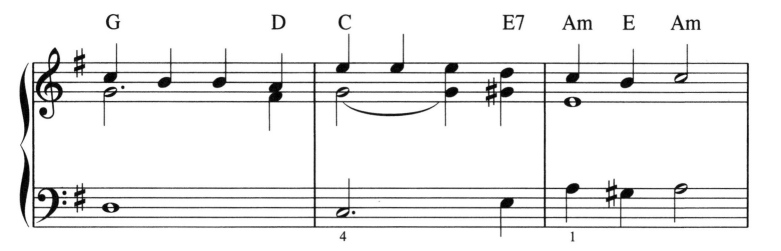

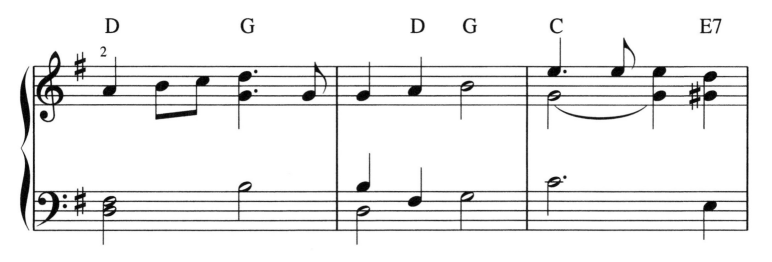

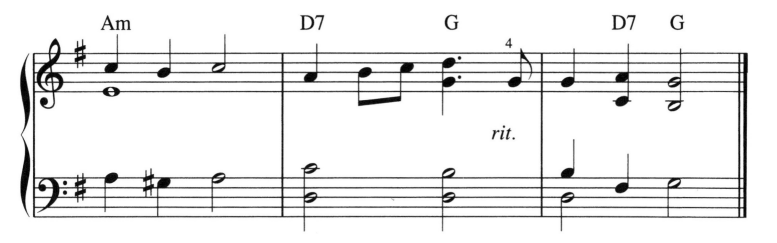

I SAW MOMMY KISSING SANTA CLAUS

Words and Music by
TOMMIE CONNOR

Moderately Slow

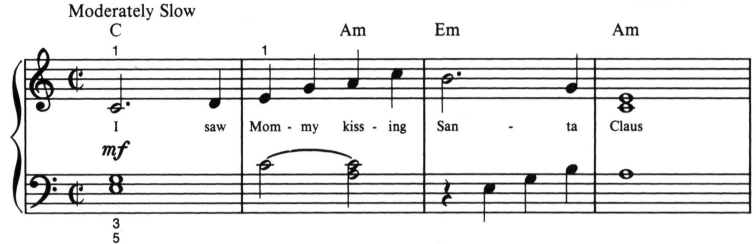

I saw Mom-my kiss-ing San - ta Claus

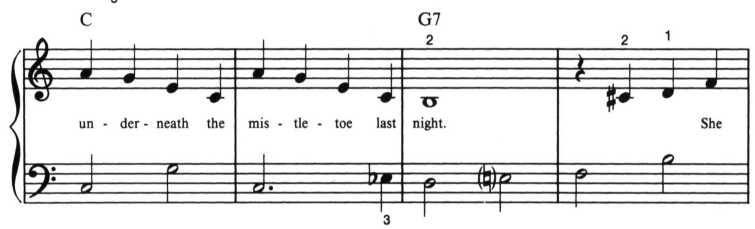

un - der-neath the mis - tle - toe last night. She

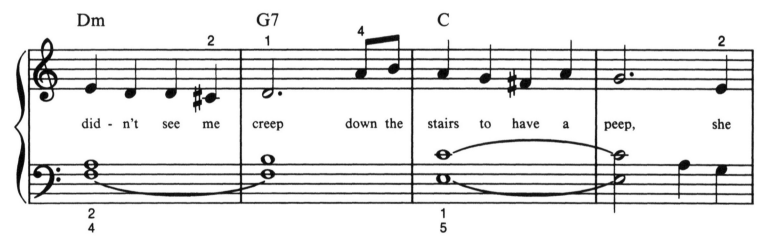

did - n't see me creep down the stairs to have a peep, she

thought that I was tucked up in my bed-room fast a - sleep. Then

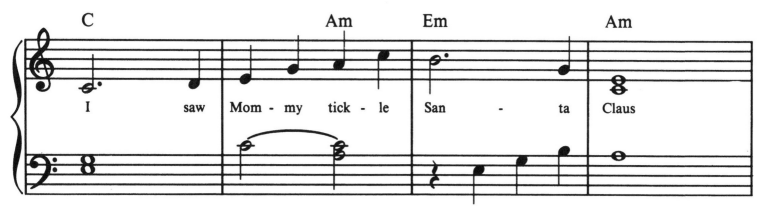

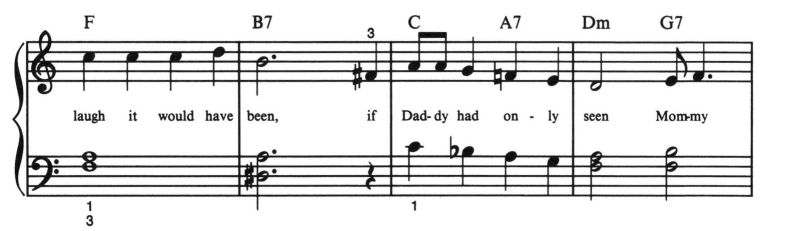

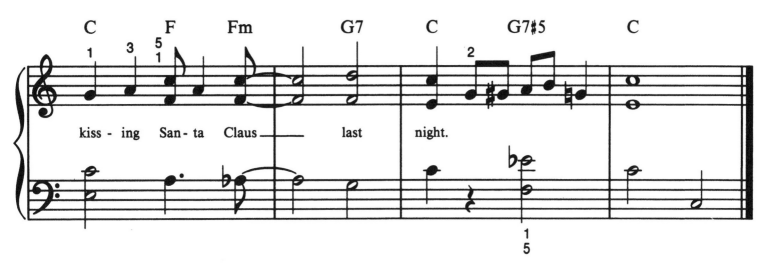

JINGLE-BELL ROCK

Words and Music by JOE BEAL
and JIM BOOTHE

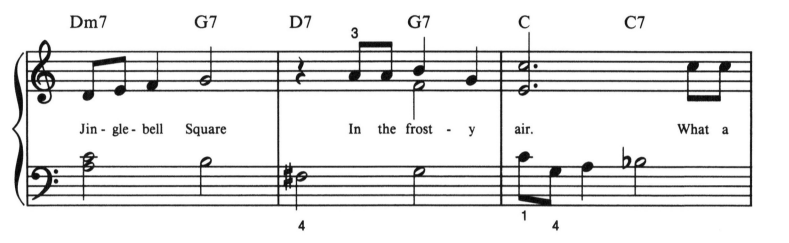

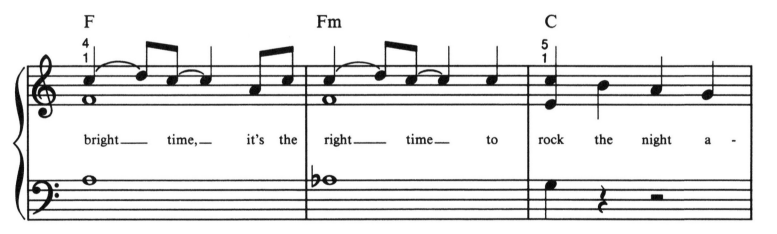

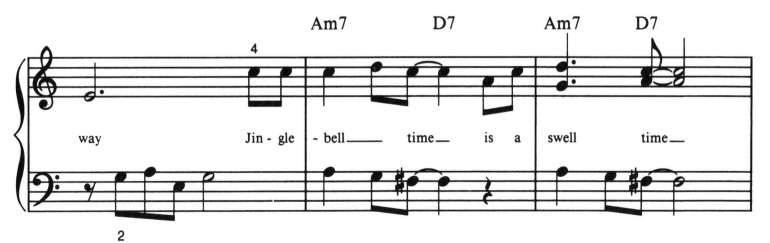

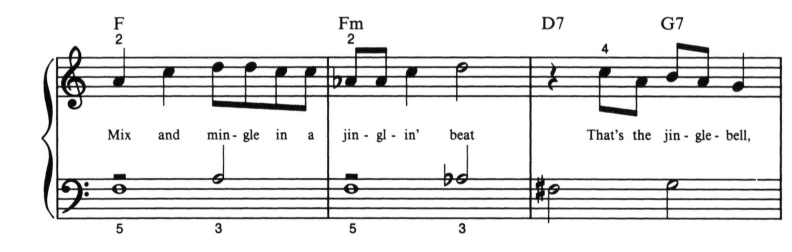

JINGLE BELLS

With Spirit

Words and Music by J. PIERPONT

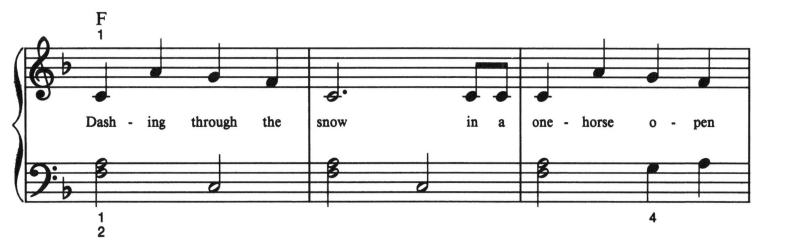

Dash - ing through the snow in a one - horse o - pen

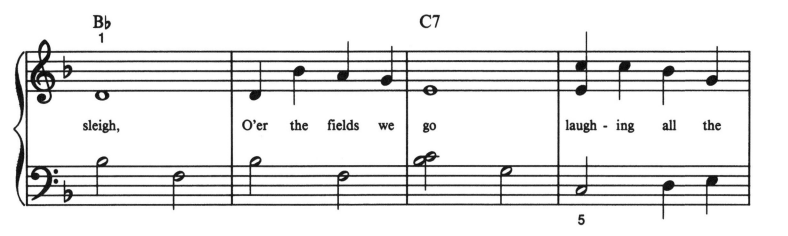

sleigh, O'er the fields we go laugh - ing all the

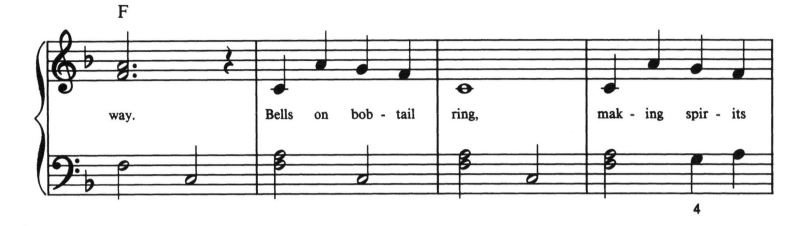

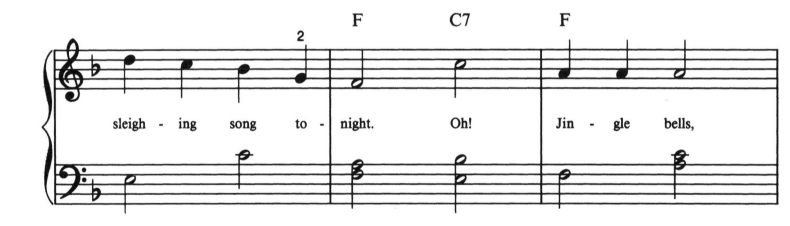

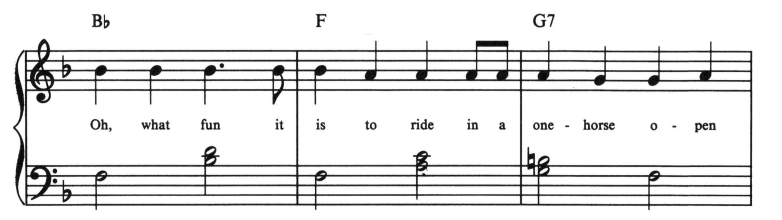

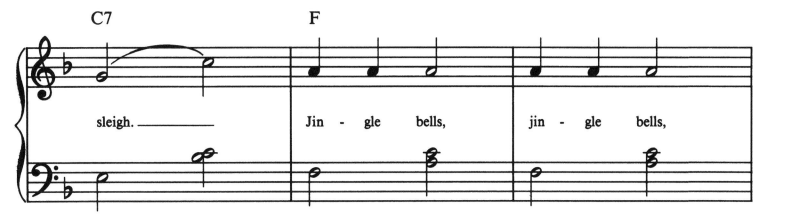

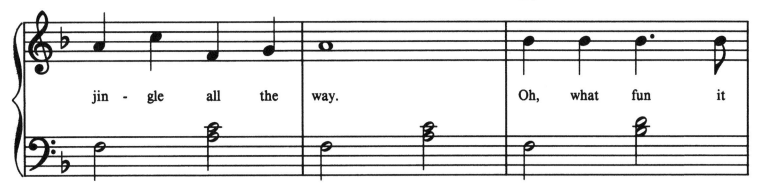

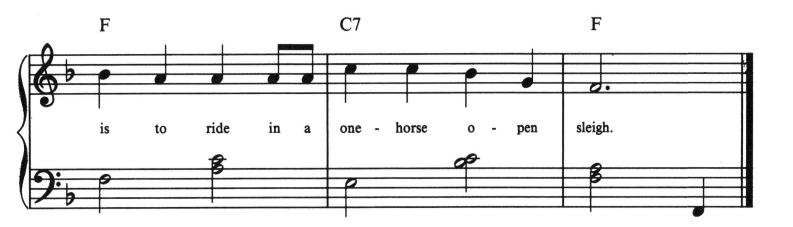

JINGLE, JINGLE, JINGLE

Music and Lyrics by
JOHNNY MARKS

Not too fast

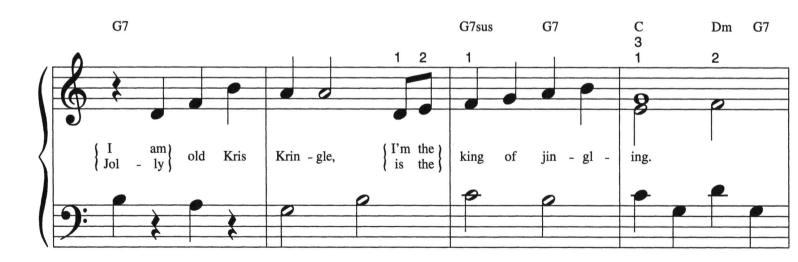

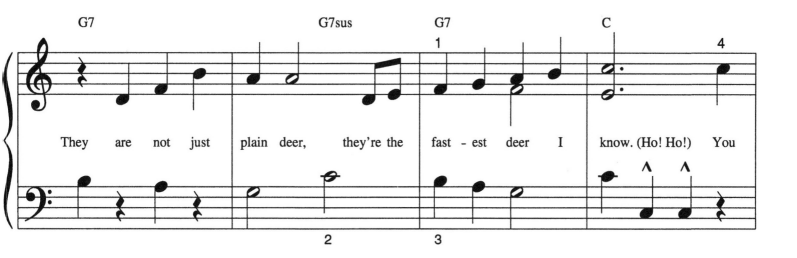

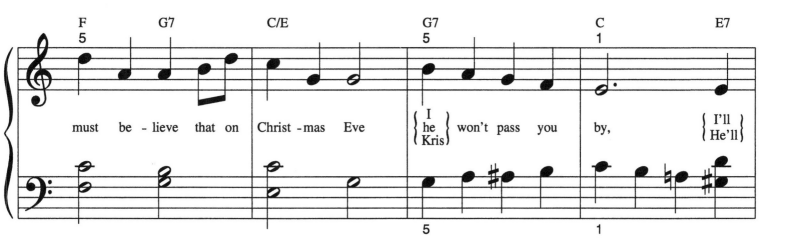

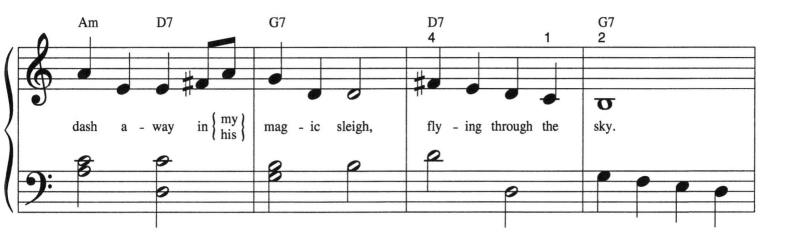

Jin - gle, jin - gle, jin - gle, you will hear { my / his } sleigh bells

ring, I am old Kris Krin - gle, { I'm / is } the

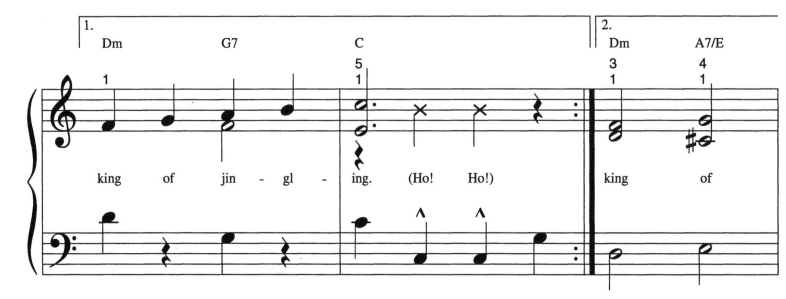

king of jin - gl - ing. (Ho! Ho!) king of

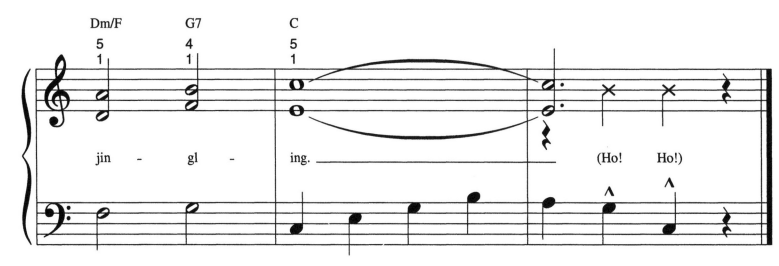

jin - gl - ing. _____ (Ho! Ho!)

JOLLY OLD ST. NICHOLAS

Moderately Slow

Traditional

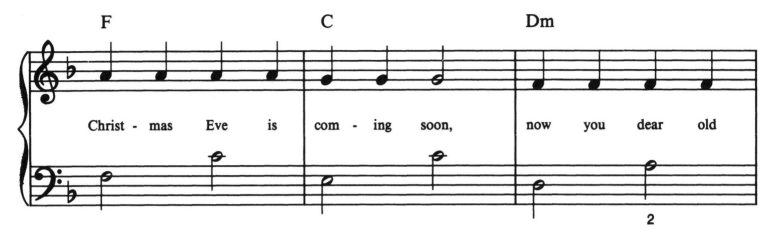

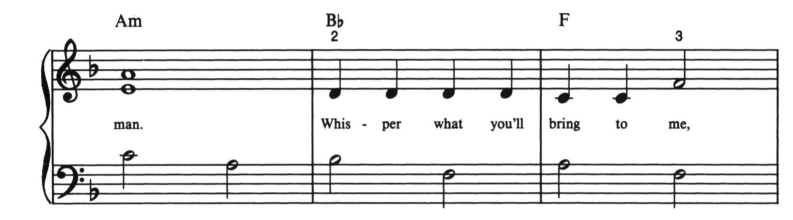

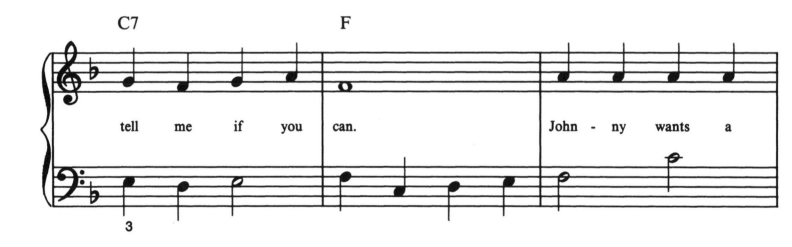

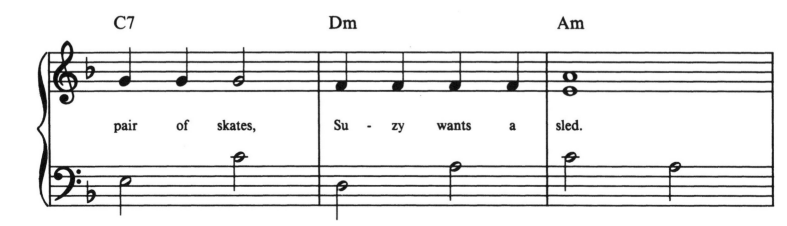

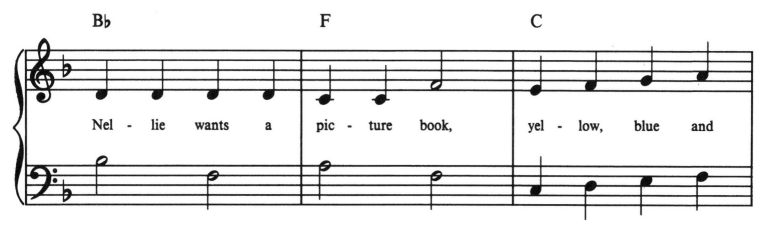

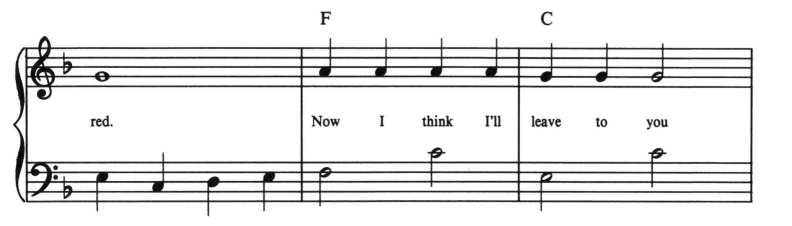

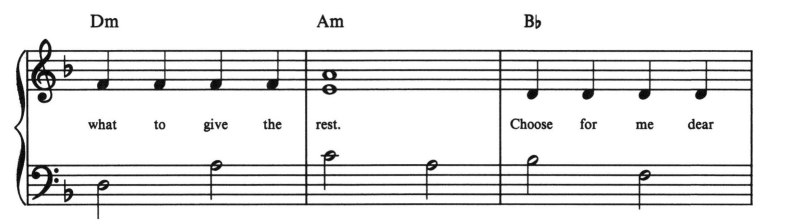

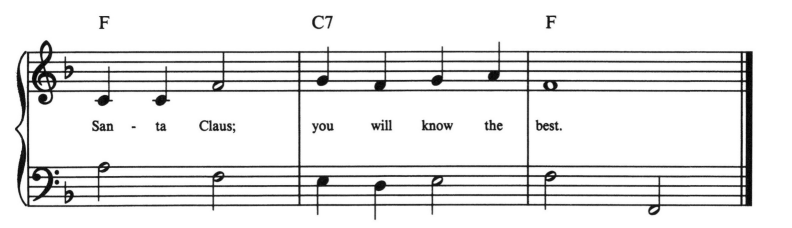

JOY TO THE WORLD

Words by ISAAC WATTS
Music by GEORGE F. HANDEL

Moderately

Joy to the world! The Lord is
He rules the world with truth and

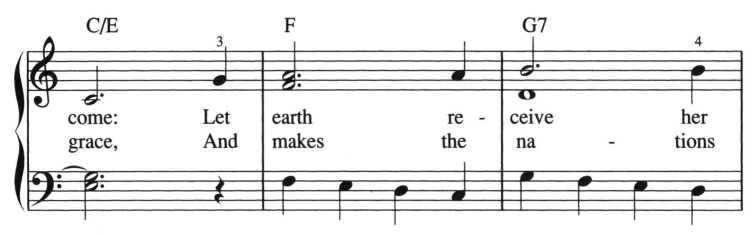

come: Let earth makes re - ceive her
grace, And the na - tions

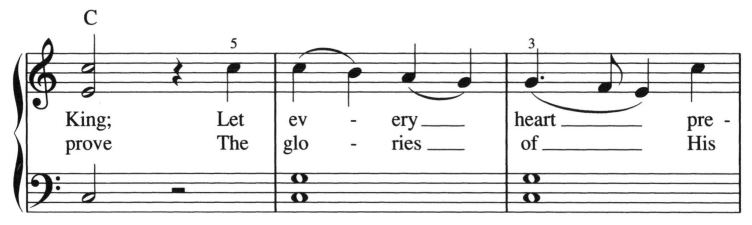

King; Let ev - ery heart pre-
prove The glo - ries of His

pare Him room, And heaven and na - ture
right - eous - ness, And won - ders of His

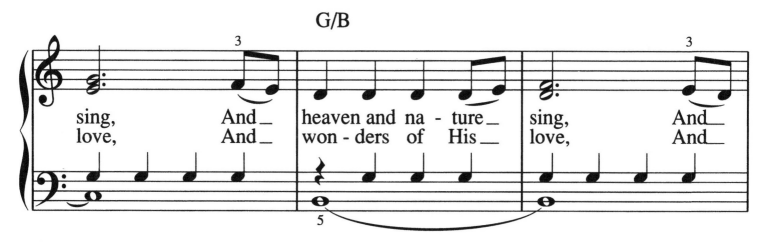

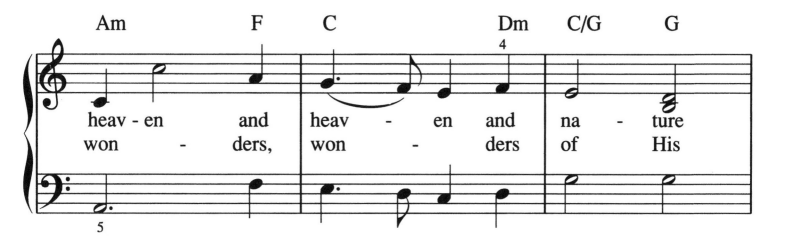

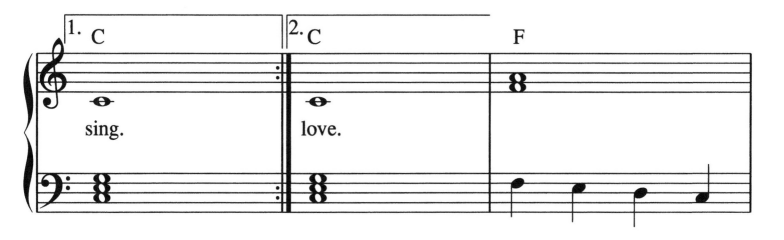

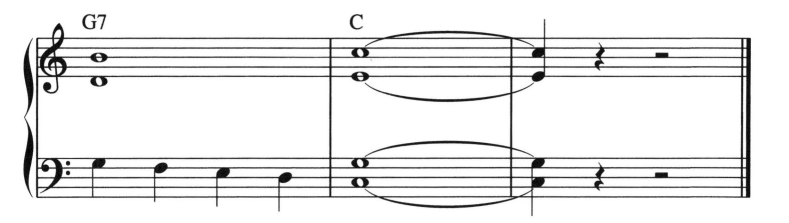

THE NIGHT BEFORE CHRISTMAS SONG

Music by JOHNNY MARKS
Lyrics adapted by JOHN MARKS
from CLEMENT MOORE'S Poem

Not too fast

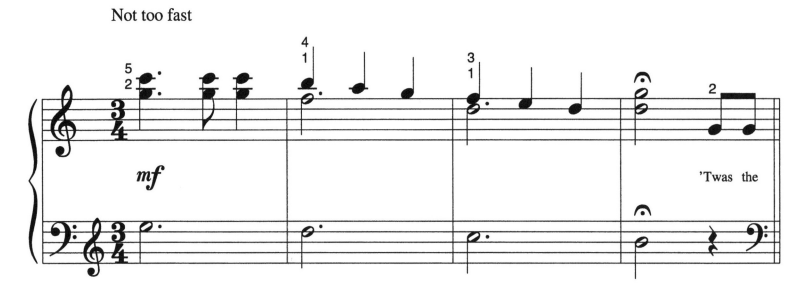

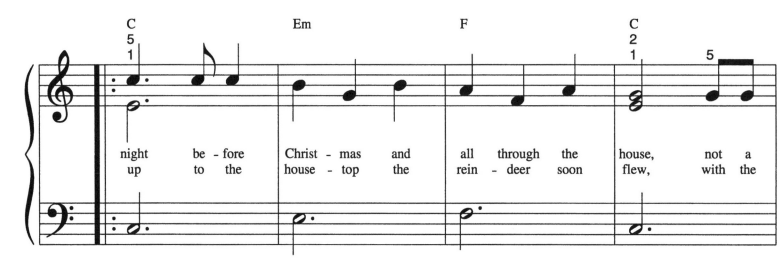

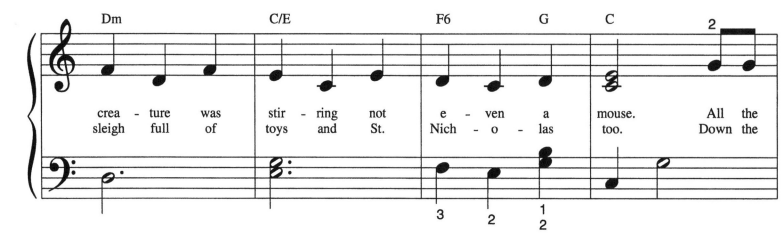

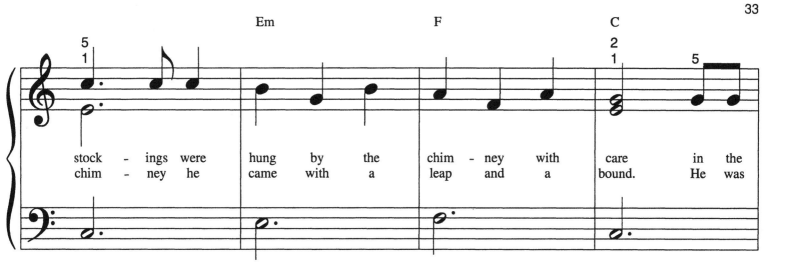

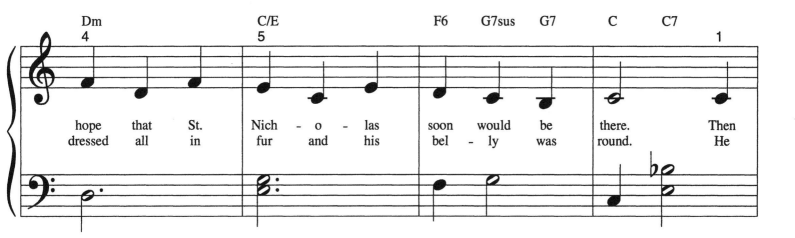

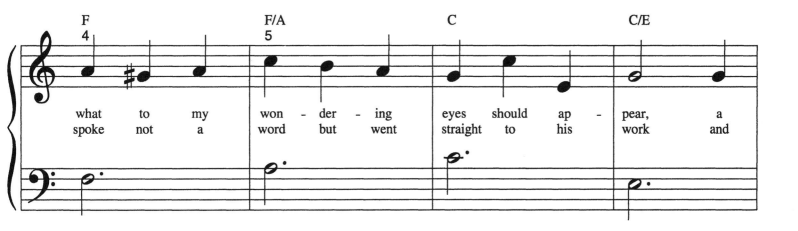

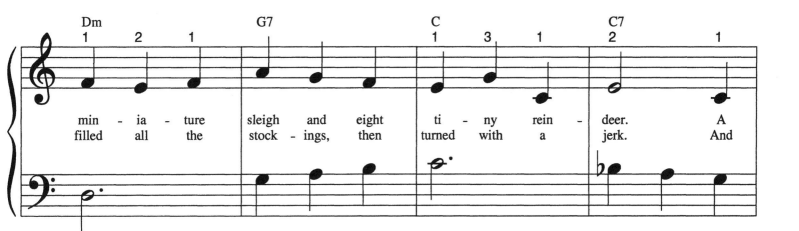

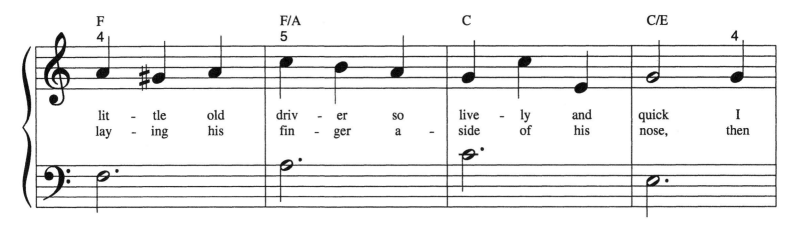

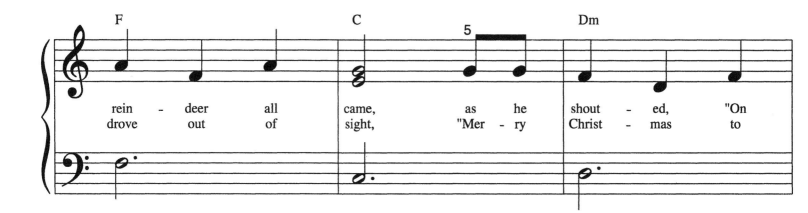

Dash – er" and each rein – deer's name.
all and to

LOOK – HERE COMES RUDOLPH!

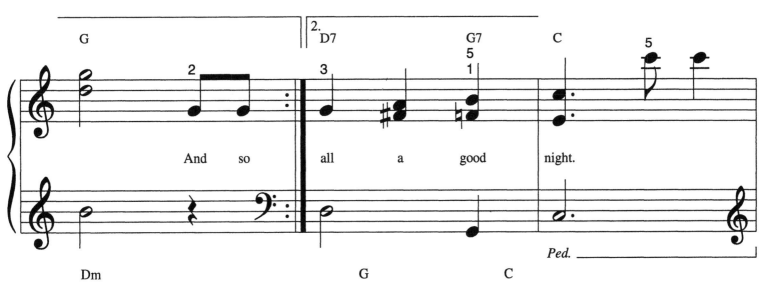

And so all a good night.

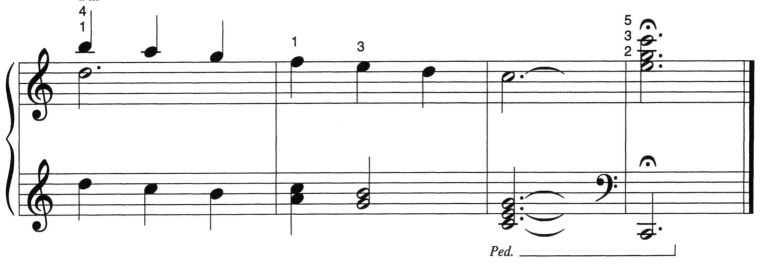

NUTTIN' FOR CHRISTMAG

Words and Music by ROY BENNETT
and SID TEPPER

Brightly

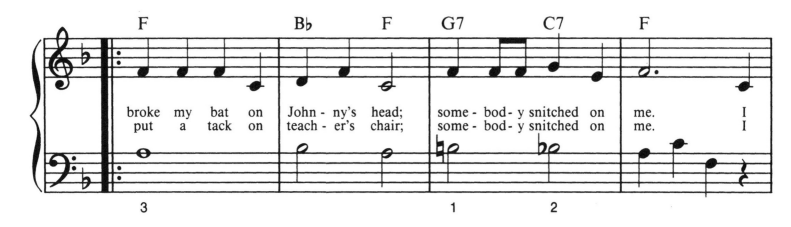

broke my bat on John-ny's head; some-bod-y snitched on me. I
put a tack on teach-er's chair; some-bod-y snitched on me. I

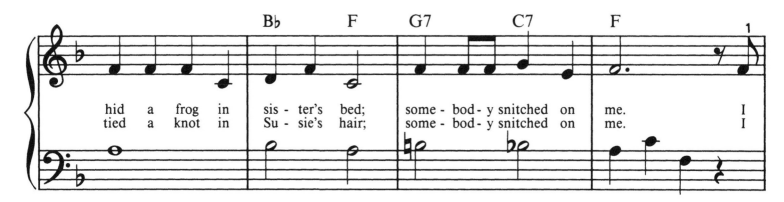

hid a frog in sis-ter's bed; some-bod-y snitched on me. I
tied a knot in Su-sie's hair; some-bod-y snitched on me. I

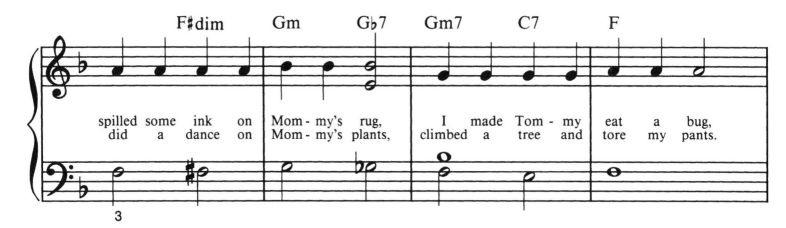

spilled some ink on Mom-my's rug, I made Tom-my eat a bug,
did a dance on Mom-my's plants, climbed a tree and tore my pants.

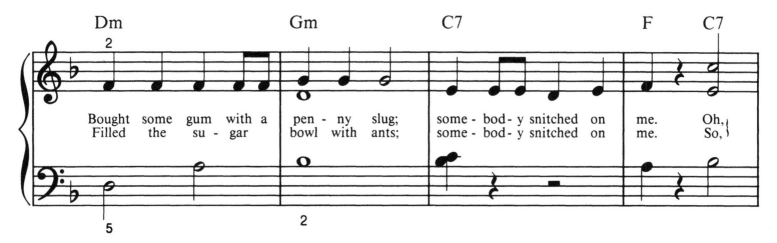

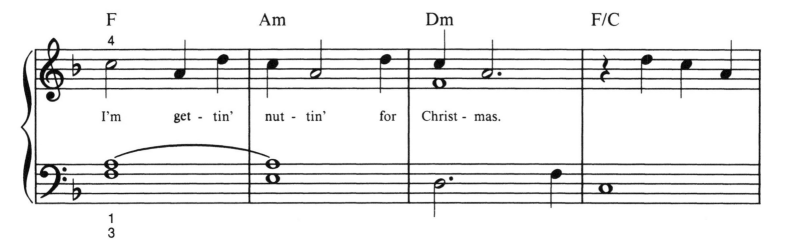

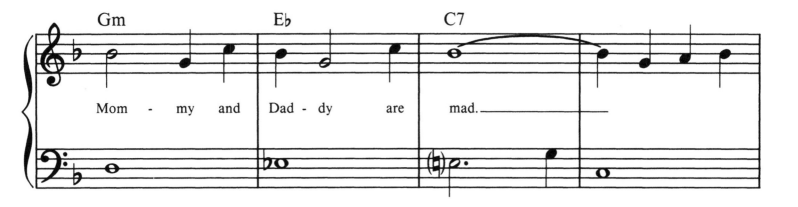

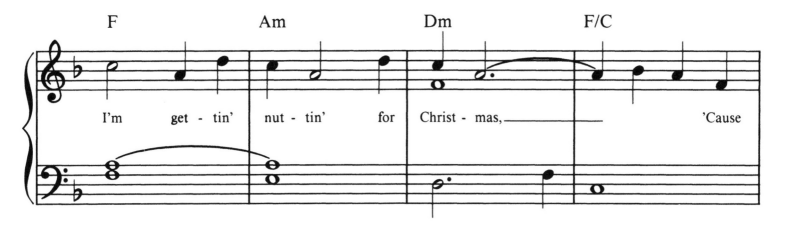

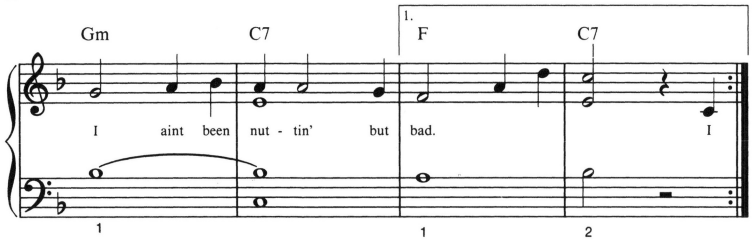

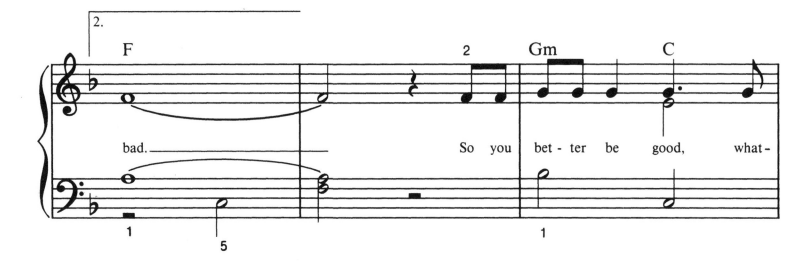

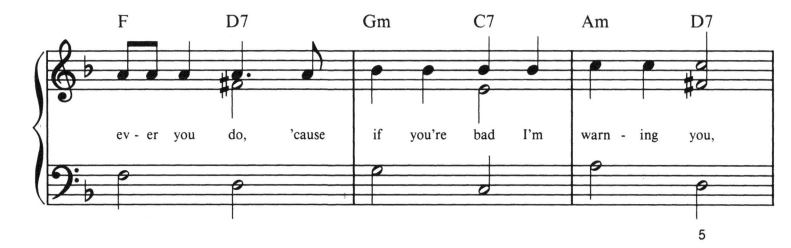

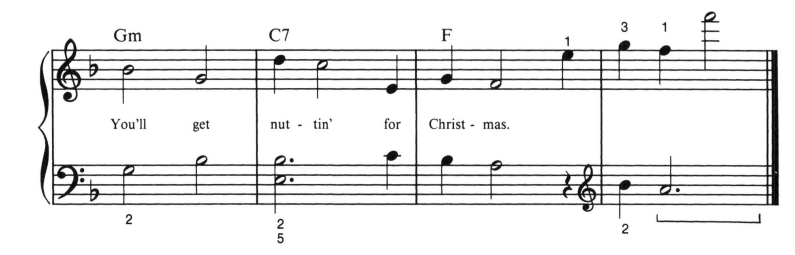

O CHRISTMAS TREE

German

Moderately Slow

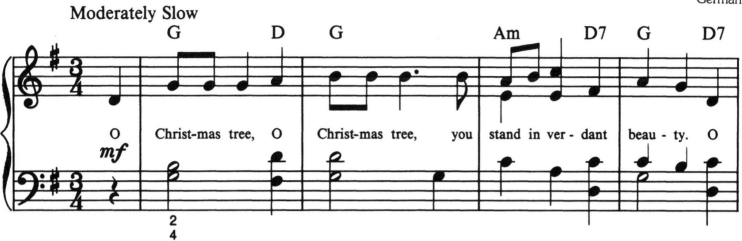

O Christ-mas tree, O Christ-mas tree, you stand in ver - dant beau - ty. O

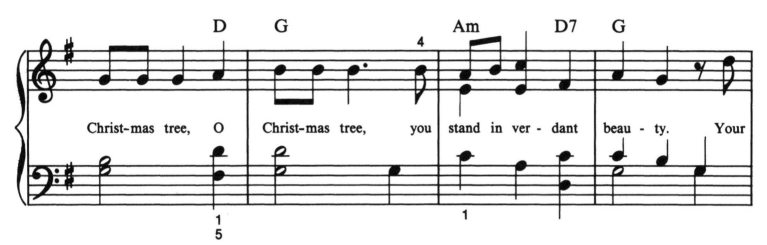

Christ-mas tree, O Christ-mas tree, you stand in ver - dant beau - ty. Your

boughs are green in sum-mer's glow And do not fade in win-ter's snow. O

Christ-mas tree, O Christ-mas tree, you stand in ver - dant beau - ty.

O LITTLE TOWN OF BETHLEHEM

Words by PHILLIP BROOKS
Music by LEWIS H. REDNER

Moderately

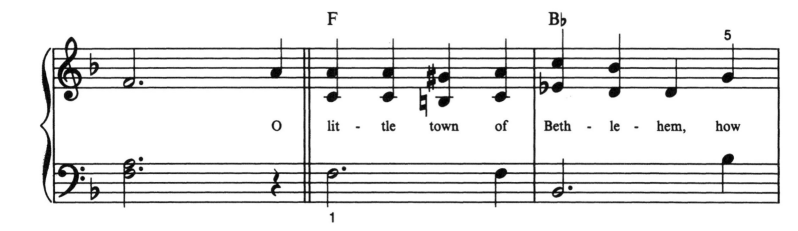

41

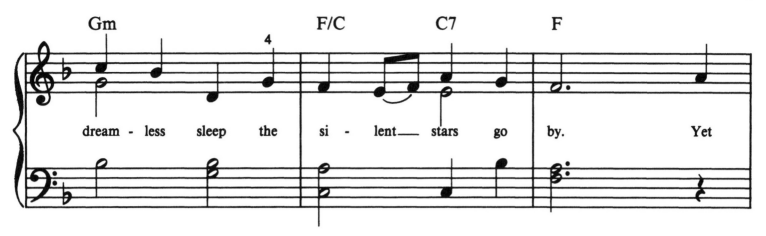

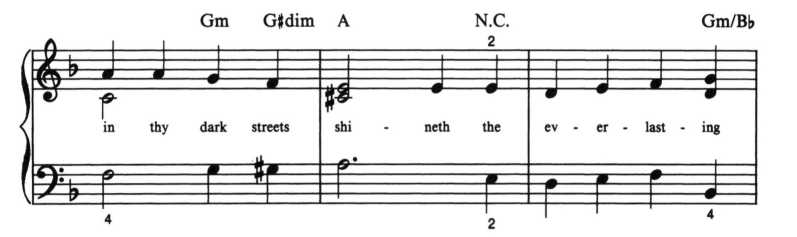

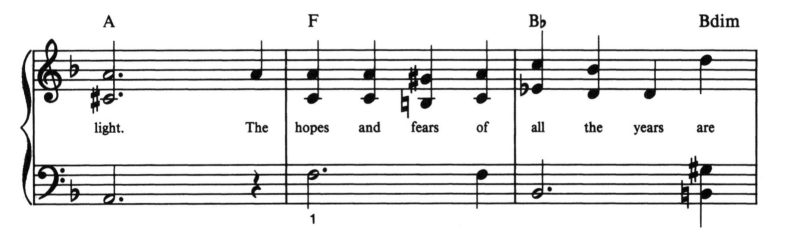

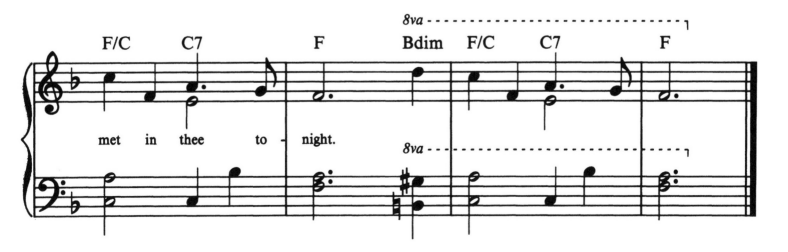

O COME ALL YE FAITHFUL

Music by JOHN READING

Moderately

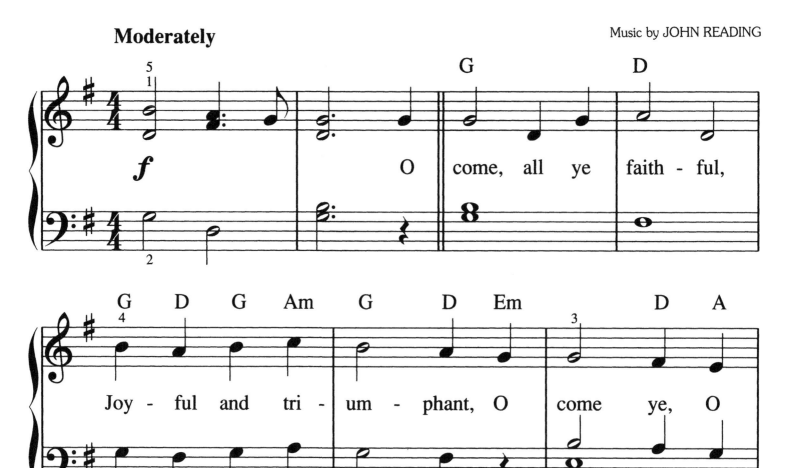

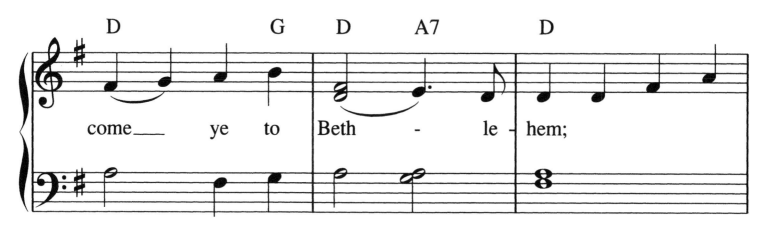

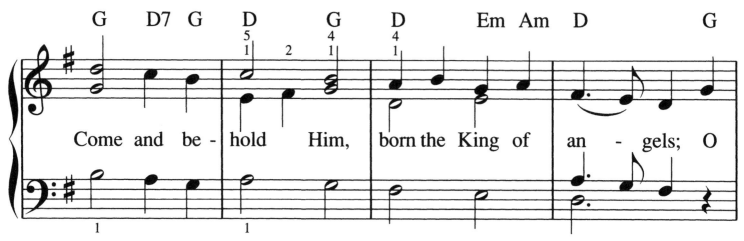

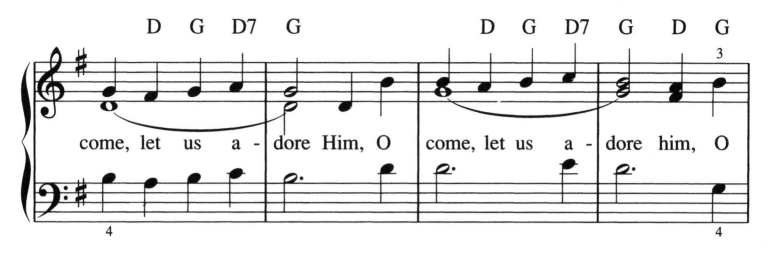

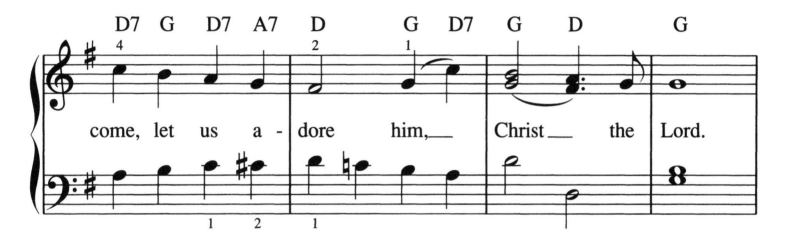

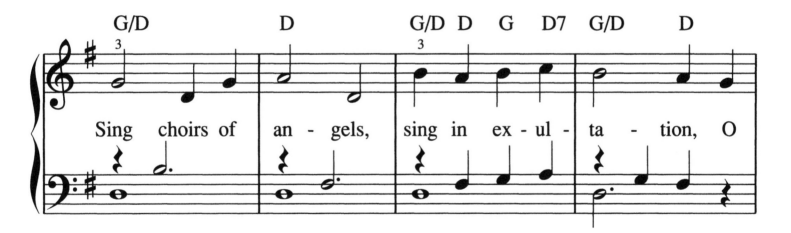

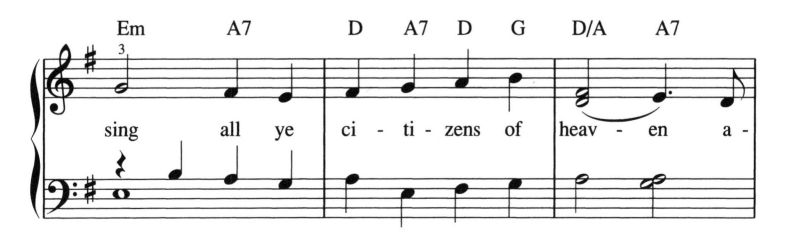

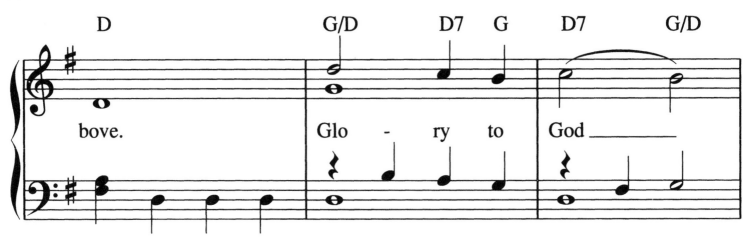

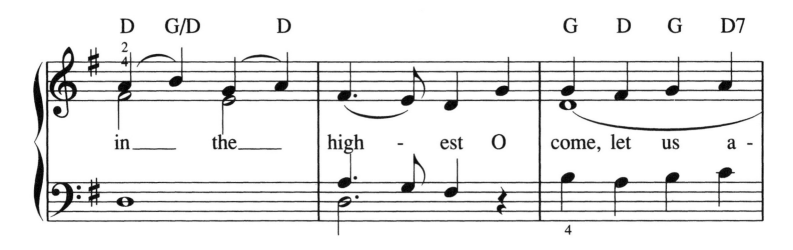

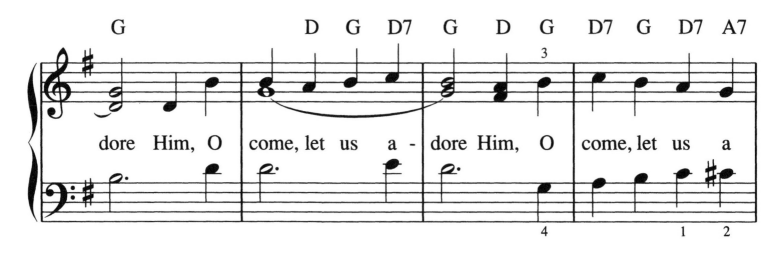

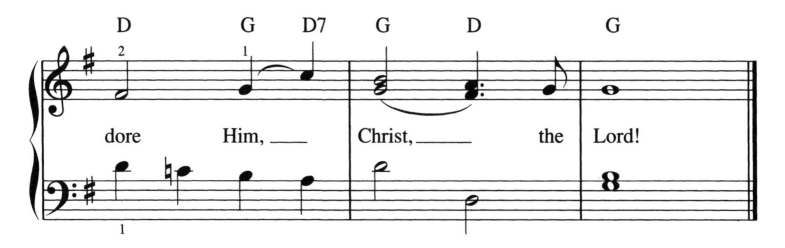

RUDOLPH, THE RED-NOSED REINDEER

Music and Lyrics by
JOHNNY MARKS

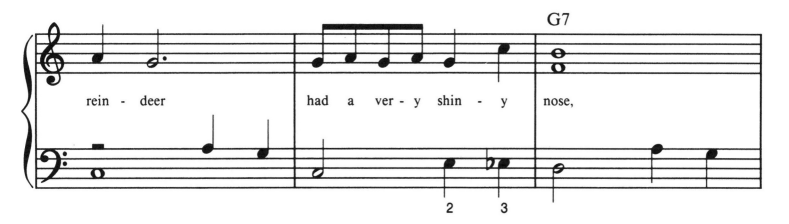

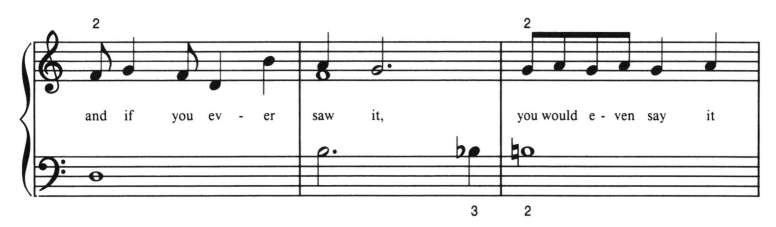

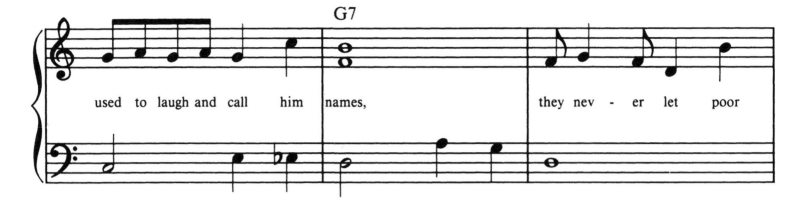

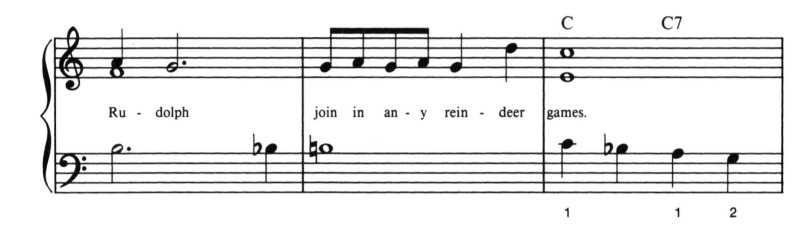

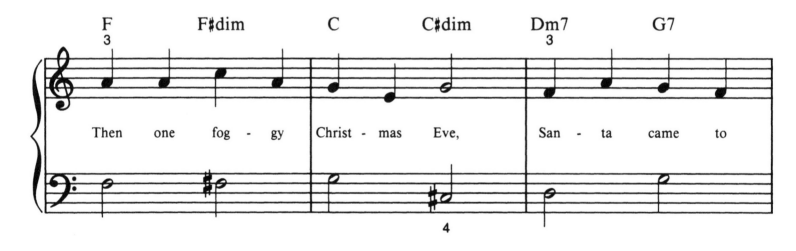

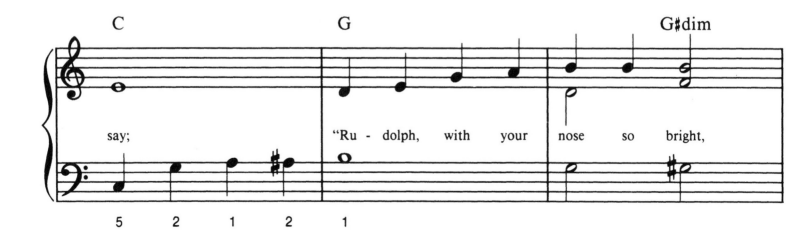

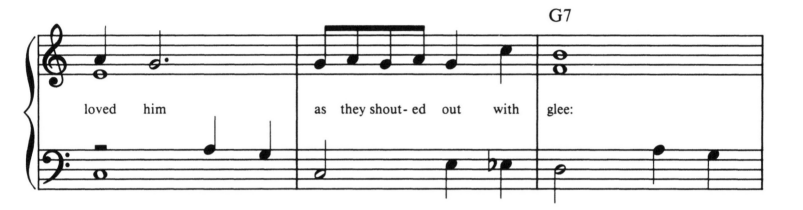

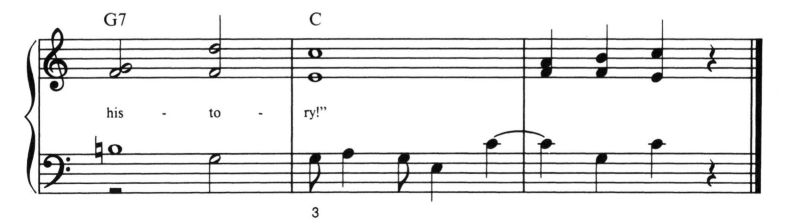

SILENT NIGHT

Words by JOSEPH MOHR
Music by FRANZ GRUBER

Quietly

Si - lent night, ho - ly night,

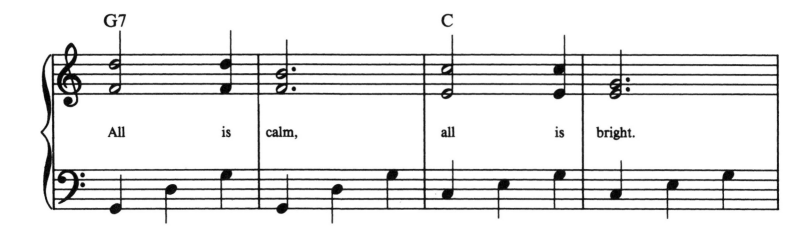

All is calm, all is bright.

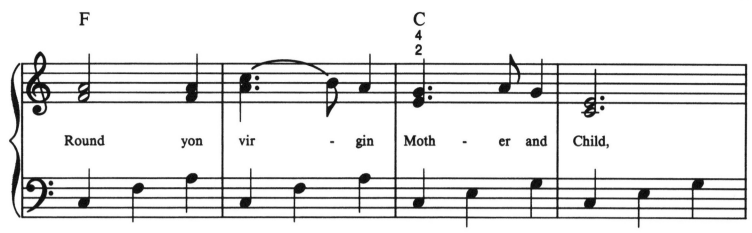

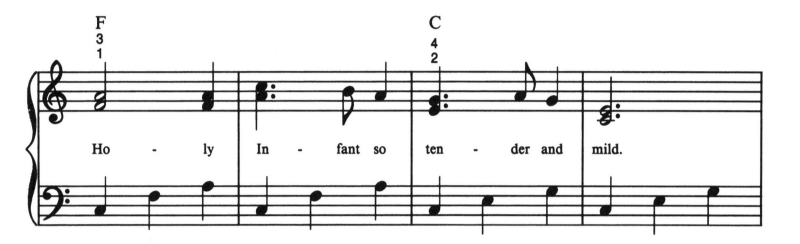

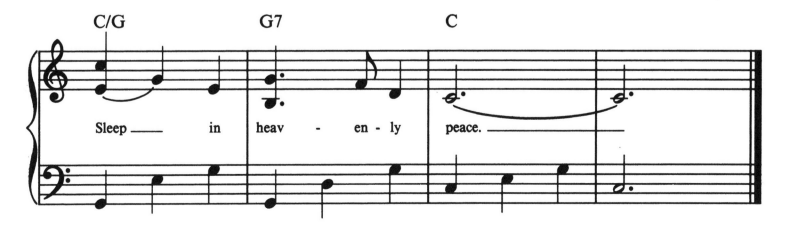

SUZY SNOWFLAKE

Moderately

Words and Music by SID TEPPER
and ROY BENNETT

Here comes

Su - zy Snow - flake, dressed in a snow - white gown,

Tap, tap tap - pin' at your win - dow pane to tell you she's in

town.

Here comes Su - zy Snow - flake,

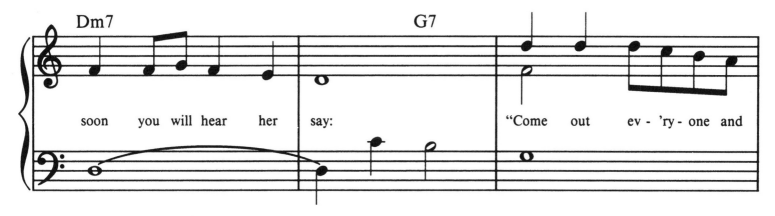

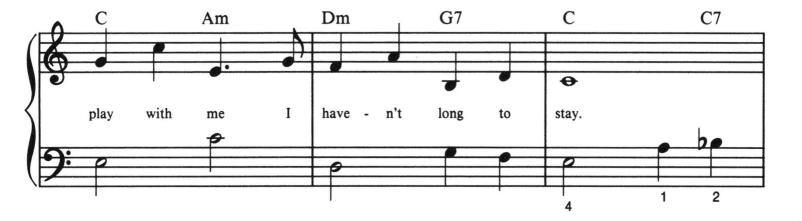

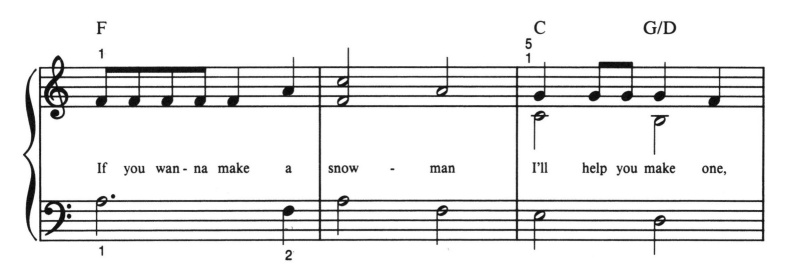

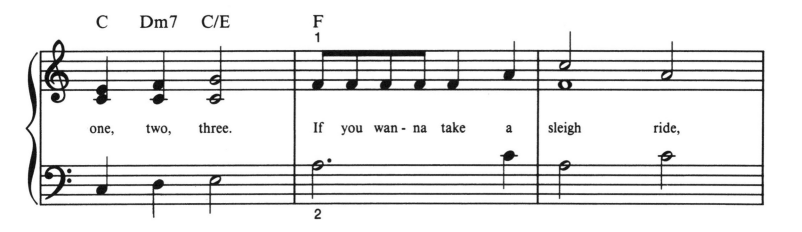

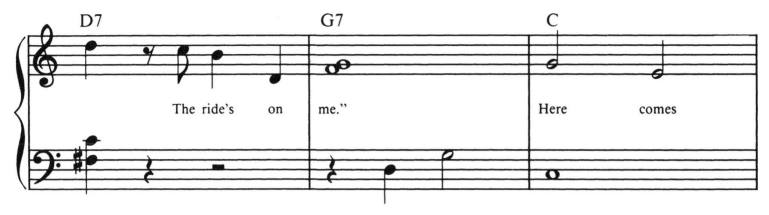

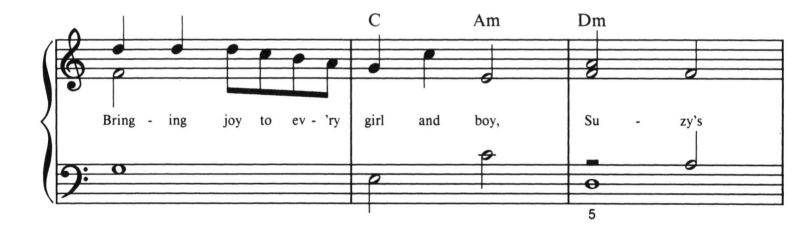

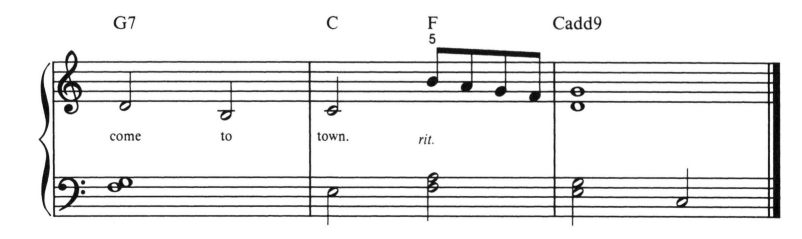

UP ON THE HOUSETOP

Brightly

Traditional

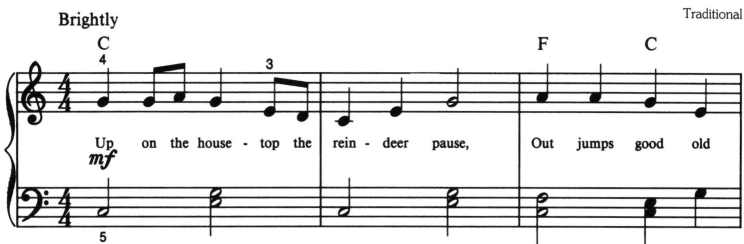

Up on the house - top the rein - deer pause, Out jumps good old

San - ta Claus; Down thru the chim - ney with lots of toys,

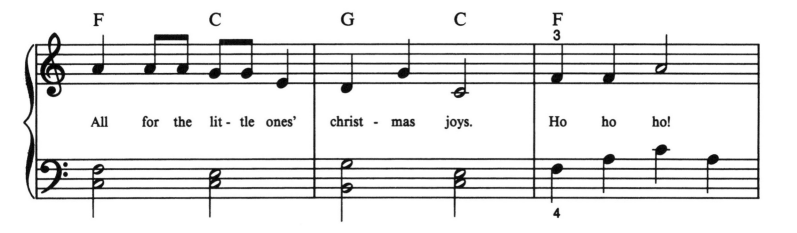

All for the lit - tle ones' christ - mas joys. Ho ho ho!

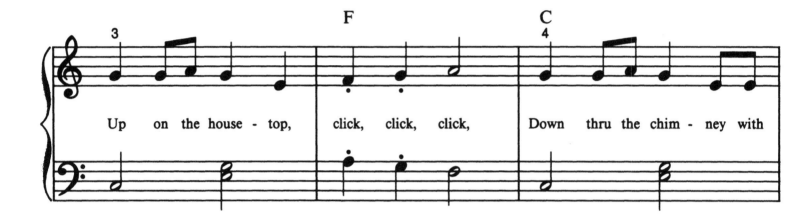

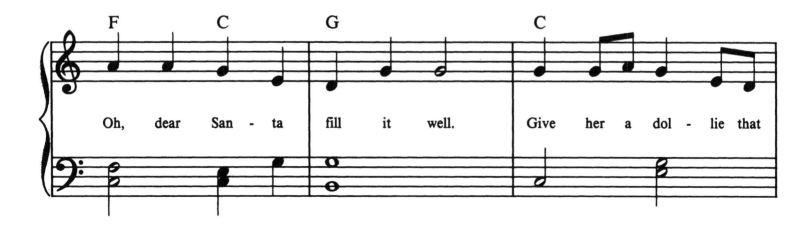

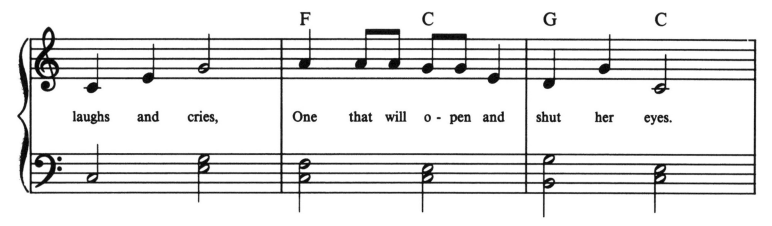

laughs and cries, One that will o - pen and shut her eyes.

Ho ho ho! Who would-n't go! Ho ho ho!

Who would-n't go ——— Up on the house top, click, click, click.

Down thru the chim - ney with good Saint Nick.

TOYLAND

Words by GLEN MacDONOUGH
Music by VICTOR HERBERT

Moderate Waltz

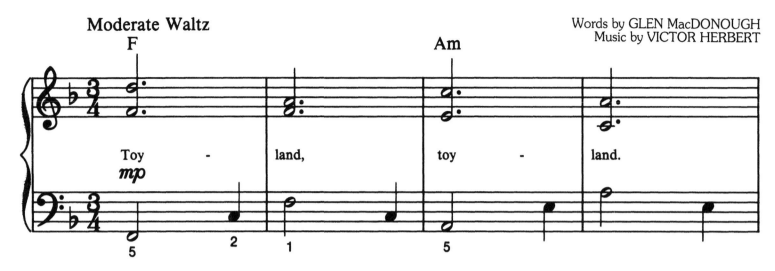

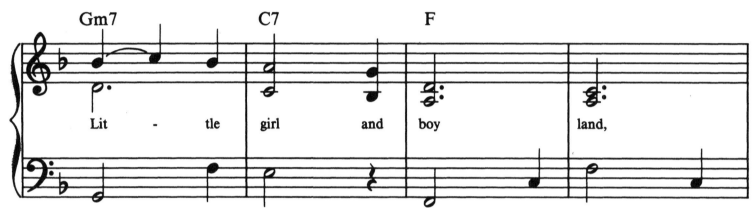

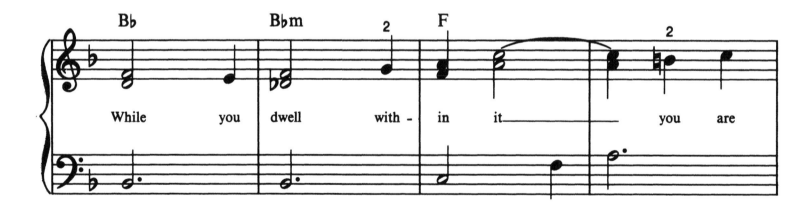

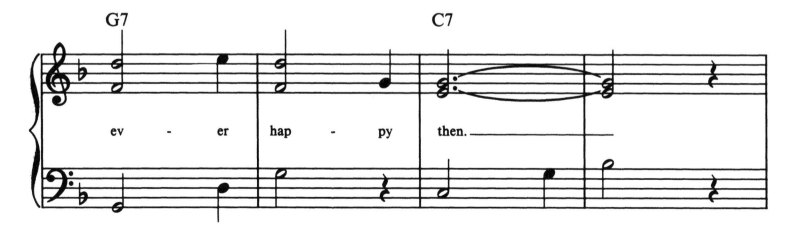

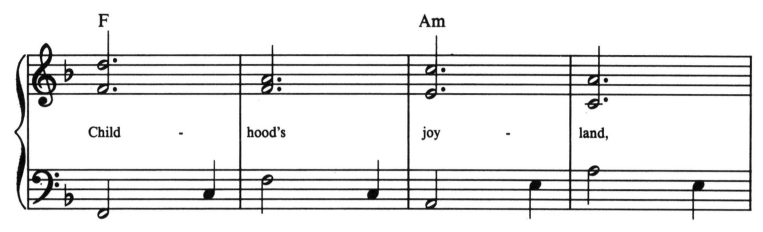

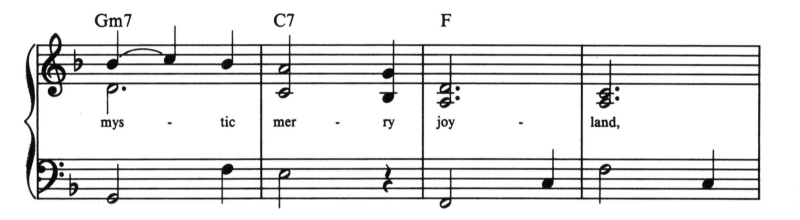

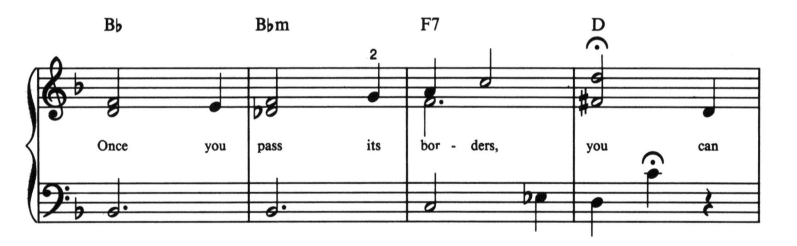

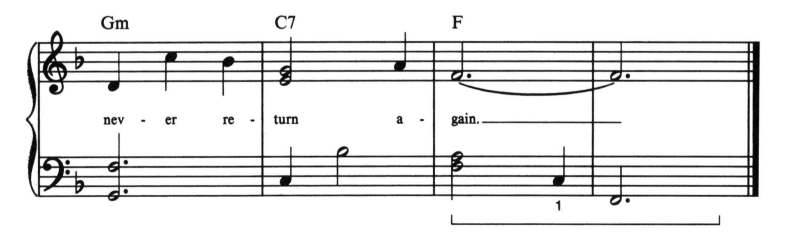

WE WISH YOU A MERRY CHRISTMAS

English

Moderately Fast

mf

We

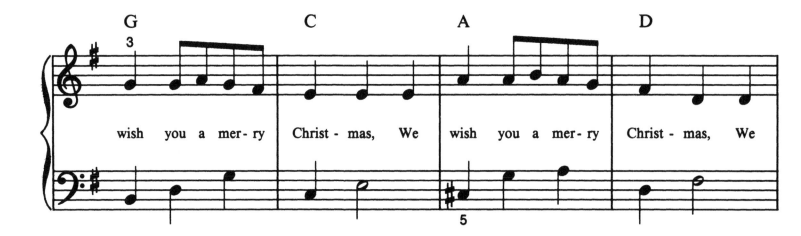

G   C   A   D

wish you a mer-ry   Christ-mas, We   wish you a mer-ry   Christ-mas, We

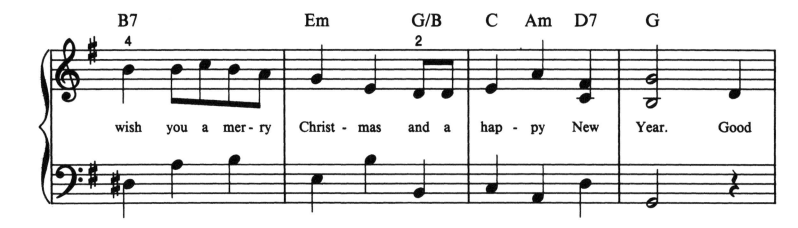

B7   Em   G/B   C Am D7   G

wish you a mer-ry   Christ-mas and a   hap-py New   Year.   Good

59

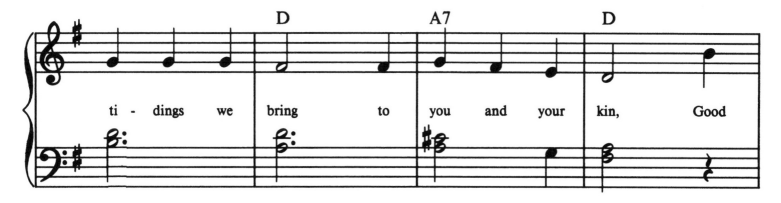

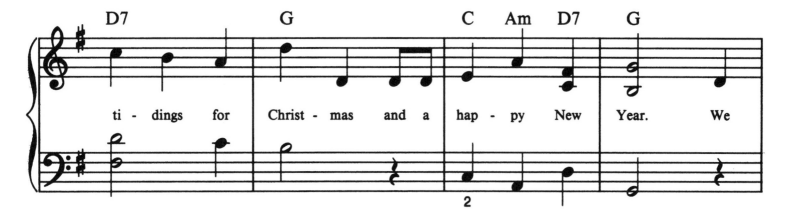

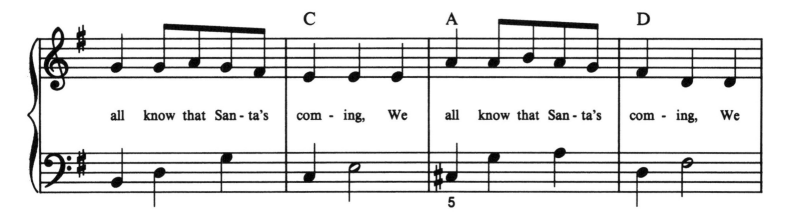

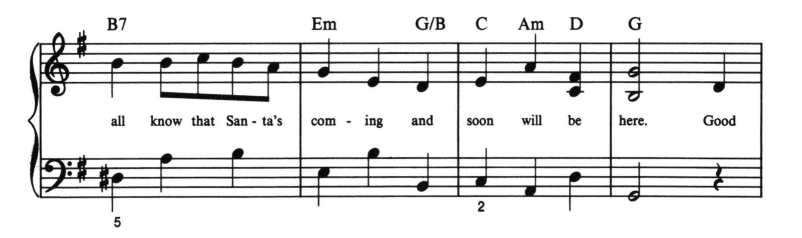

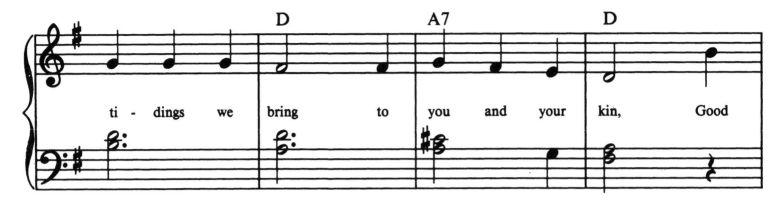

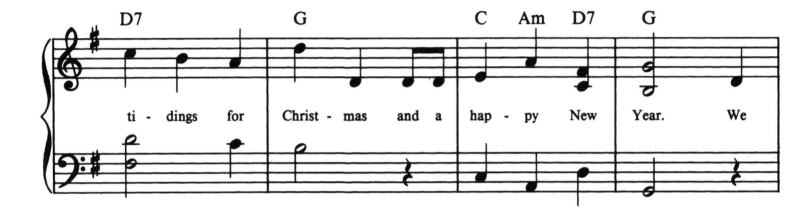

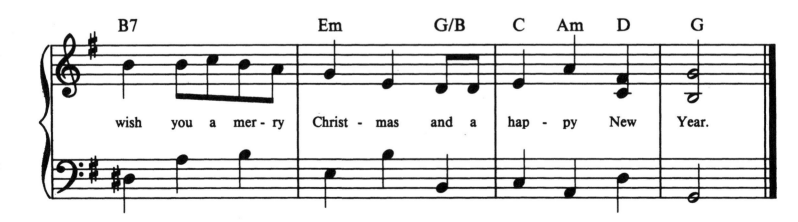

WHEN SANTA CLAUS GETS YOUR LETTER

Music and Lyrics by
JOHNNY MARKS

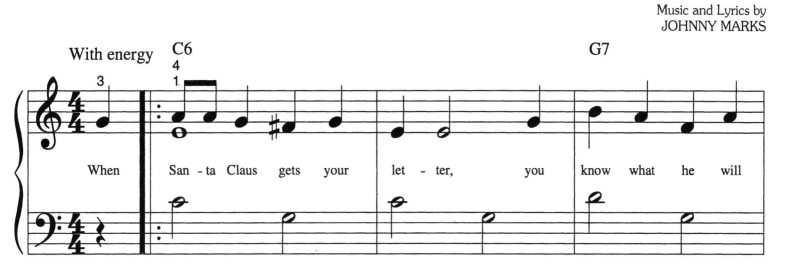

When San - ta Claus gets your let - ter, you know what he will

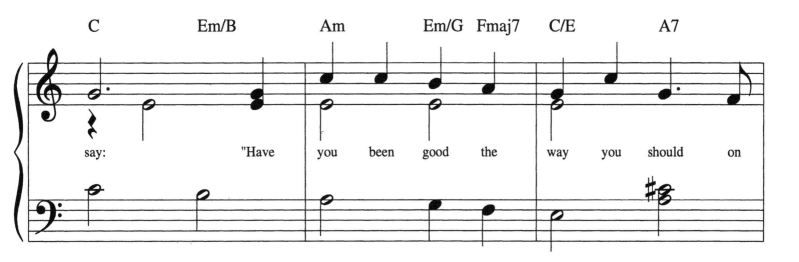

say: "Have you been good the way you should on

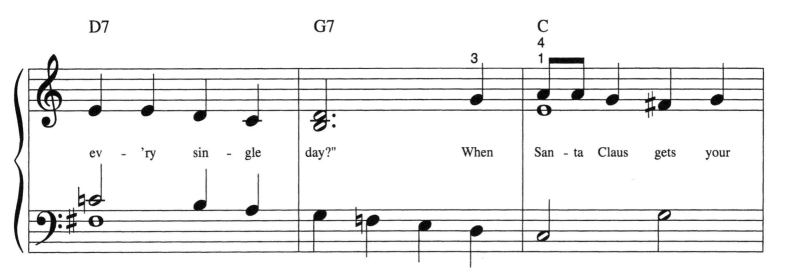

ev - 'ry sin - gle day?" When San - ta Claus gets your

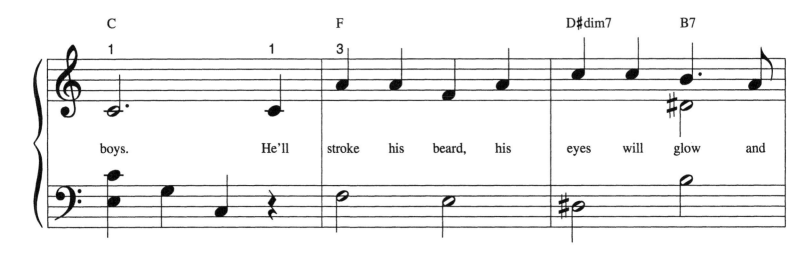

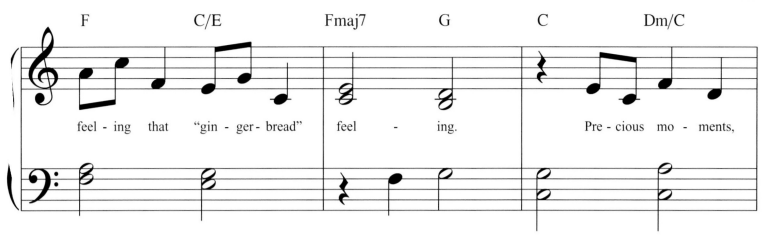

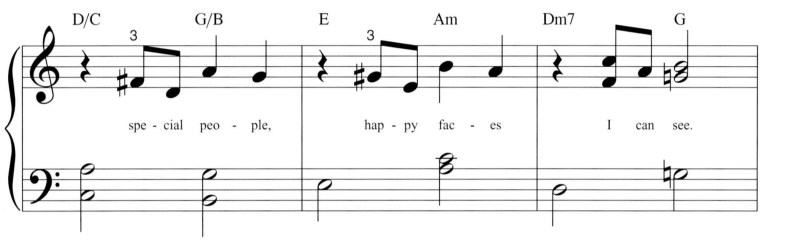

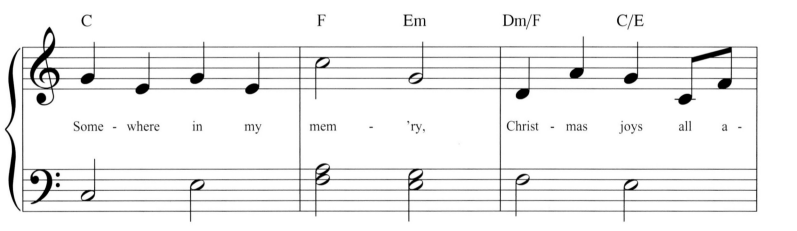

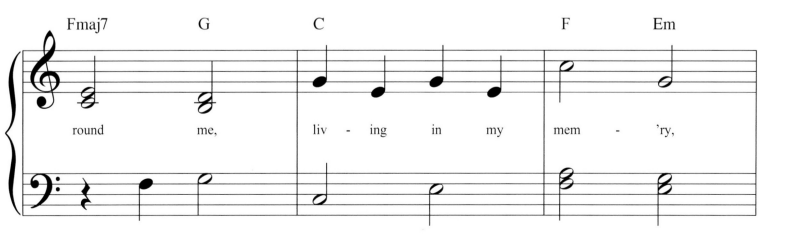

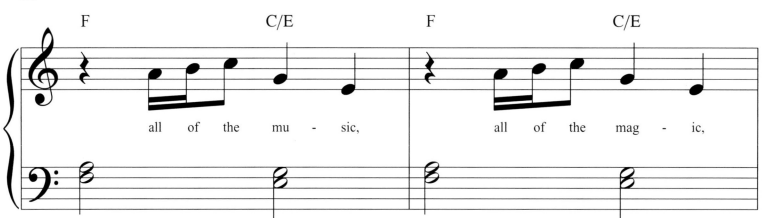

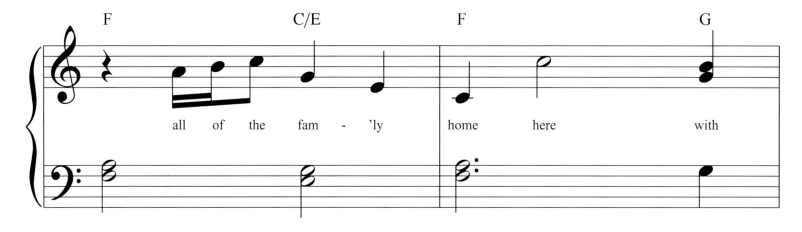

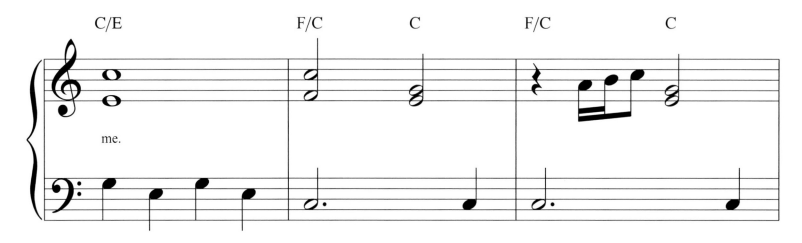

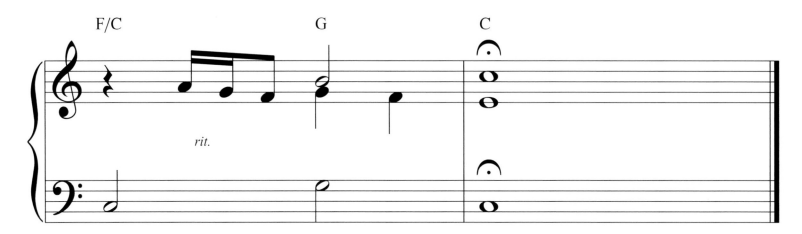